MW01613444

Free

How to
Stop Struggling
and
Start Living

Rebecca K. Merriman

RIDGETOP PUBLISHING

Other books by Rebecca K. Merriman

Simply Happy:
    How to Simplify Your Life and Find Happiness

Editor, Vicki Gill
Cover Design, Tad Crisp
Design/production, TypeByte Graphix

Library of Congress Catalog Card Number 98-84142

ISBN 1-891825-00-3

RidgeTop Publishing
7101 Old 31 East
Nashville, TN 37186
615-644-4624
e-mail TypeByte@aol.com

Contents

Preface

Many years ago I read an article in *Architectural Digest* about a happy, successful author who spent each winter in his exquisite, palm-fringed villa high above the sparkling Caribbean. I don't remember the author's name or the particular island, but what I do remember is the freedom the author had created for himself. He was doing what he loved, living where he wanted, and making the world a happier place because of it.

I began wondering what freedom felt like. What were the secrets to creating a life filled with purpose, passion and liberty?

I'm sure you've wondered, too. Otherwise life wouldn't have brought you to this place, this moment, this book. If hopeless circumstances, uninspiring work or too many distracting obligations have you feeling bound, then take heart!

What follows is your blueprint for creating

a life of freedom and joy. The simple steps contained herein have one purpose: To unshackle your self-imposed chains of limitation and fear —to set you free!

If you've ever caught yourself dreaming of more freedom, this little treasure chest of practical steps is all you need to unlock what's already inside you. As the Buddhist aphorism says:

> *You have come here to find*
> *what you already have.*

You were born to be free. My wish is that you find your way back to your rightful inheritance.

1   Simply Free

*...and I blessed God that I was free
to wander, free to hope and free to
love.*   —Robert Louis Stevenson

Do you sometimes feel you are a victim
of circumstances? A prisoner locked in a
lifestyle you find limiting and uninspiring?
If you are a captive who dreams of freedom... this little book is just for you.

You see, I've been where you are. A few
years ago I found myself trapped in a job
that no longer inspired me. Rather than
looking forward to each day with anticipation and excitement—as in the past—I
awoke with dread. It got so bad, in fact,
that some Monday mornings I cried all the
way to work.

One saving grace was that I had already learned the value of rising one hour earlier each morning to get centered for the day. Soulful journal writing, prayer, meditation and an uplifting reading of some sort were the medicines that kept me healthy during this trying time. This daily early morning ritual led me to the truths contained in the pages of this little guide-book to freedom. But first, let's finish the story...

For five years I relished my work as an award-winning high school teacher. The challenges and rewards of reaching "un-reachable" teenagers kept me enriched and fulfilled. I loved my students and my job. But the 6th year was different. I still loved the kids, but somehow the job was no longer enough.

I had just spent my second summer in blissful solitude high in the Colorado Rocky Mountain wilderness; savoring precious time alone for reflection, self-discovery, spiritual growth, long hikes, soul-writing, meditation, paying attention and generally

learning how to simply *be*. As one of my favorite authors, Wayne W. Dyer, says, I was
becoming a human *being* rather than a
human doing.

With each passing week, I grew more
and more accustomed to the peace and
quiet. By the end of my second summer of
solitude I knew my life was changing from
the inside out, but had no idea how my
work would "suffer." This word is in quota-
tions because now I know such a negative
term is purely a subjective judgment. One
of the truths we'll cover in these pages: To
rise to a higher level of living, we must
stop judging situations as "bad" or "good"
—they just ARE.

Back to the story: Totally invigorated,
inspired and refreshed, I started that
school year with eager anticipation. Well,
the first thing I noticed was the incredible
amount of high volume noise. In a high
school overflowing with thirteen hundred
bustling teenagers, I'm sure this intoler-
able noise had merely escaped my atten-

tion the previous five years. Had I become so accustomed to the blissful quietness of the mountains that I could no longer handle the inevitable clamor of the booming hallways?

By the 5th week, all one hundred and forty seven of my students knew without a doubt that I accepted and loved them unconditionally, and that I had very high expectations of them. But they had no idea the turmoil going on inside their teacher.

By November I faced each new day with dread. One particular Monday morning, I awoke to the normal 4:30 buzzing of my alarm clock. The familiar foreboding enveloped me as I made my way into the morning. Within 20 minutes, I knew something had to give or I might just lose my mind. So, I intuitively walked out into the cold, still-dark morning.

As tears streamed down, I looked up into the star-filled sky. The frustration and confusion welled up inside and I cried out, "God, I'm begging you... Set me free!"

What happened next was something I never expected, but have come to recognize as a turning point. As clear as crystal a small voice said, "You **ARE** free!"

Shock and peace occurred simultaneously. Shocked that the undeniable answer had come so instantaneously, yet at the same moment a soothing wave of precious peace washed over me. It was the most peace I'd felt since my time in Colorado.

As I pondered the liberation of those words, I noticed for the first time the brilliance of the shimmering stars above. The galaxies of glistening gems verified what I knew those words meant: I was completely and undeniably free to live the life of my choosing. Suddenly I experienced a shift from captivity consciousness to *freedom consciousness*.

That was several years ago. Today I live a very different life. I finished that school year with a new appreciation for my students, realizing they would be my last.

Shortly after resigning, my first book was published and I was on the road to realizing my dream of freedom. Freedom from fear, debt and doubt.

Actually, freedom is realized first and foremost as a result of a perception shift, rather than by any particular events that evolve. Freedom is a journey, a state of mind, rather than a destination.

On the journey I took several simple steps that helped me to begin realizing my freedom almost immediately. However, having found joy in the journey, it wouldn't have mattered how much time had passed. Peace of mind is a delicious side effect of the ideas brought forth here. I urge you to use these simple, yet powerful, steps as the keys to unlock your self-imposed prison of doubt and fear.

In the 1938 classic by Ernest Holmes, *The Science of Mind,* we are reminded of the Truth which sets us free:

> *The Divine Plan is one of Freedom; bondage is not God-ordained. Freedom*

*is the birthright of every living soul. All
instinctively feel this.*

The journey to freedom is essentially a
spiritual path, so the word *God* appears
ubiquitously throughout this work. For
some of you this may be unsettling—bring-
ing up unpleasant, vengeful or unbeliev-
able ideas about the God of your childhood.
Please be open-minded. You will soon see
that the concept of God contained herein is
one of unconditional love and acceptance.

If you still feel uncomfortable with the
word God, feel free to substitute *Universe,
Spirit, Flow, Force, Mind, Higher Power...*
whatever is comfortable for you. In her
bestseller on creativity, *The Artist's Way,*
Julia Cameron puts it like this:

*The point is not what you name it.
The point is that you try* [trusting] *it.*

The simple truth is that living a free
life, like any other spiritual endeavor, is *ex-
periential.* Until you try trusting the concept of a beneficent creator you will not re-

alize the freedom found in this user-friend-
ly universe which is forever at your disposal.

Accepting your inborn right to freedom
is like running a marathon. You begin by
slowly, (actually much sooner that you
might imagine), gaining strength and confidence through steadfast training and exercise. This little book is your training
schedule. Your daily practice of the curriculum herein enables you to accept your
freedom.

Practiced faithfully these keys can unlock the prison of a limiting perception. By
applying the simple principles herein you
will experience the shift in perception that
is required for *freedom consciousness*.
Come with me and see how effortlessly and
joyfully you can become **Simply Free.**

2   Simply Imagine

*Let your imagination soar, for it is
your soul's blueprint for success.*
       —Sarah Ban Breathnach

The starry morn of my Freedom Revelation was the beginning of a new era for me. I had been assured of my inherent right to freedom, now what on earth was I going to do about it?

Just knowing that the choice was mine, (of how to live my life), set me free to begin seeing a higher vision of myself. With my new *freedom consciousness*, I could finally believe the words of Christ, *"Nothing shall be impossible to you."* So why not envision an abundant life full of meaning and freedom?

I began imagining in detail the life I

wanted to lead. Shortly thereafter, a dear
friend loaned me a wonderful book called
Creative Visualization by Shakti Gawain.
I urge you to read its powerful message.
Gawain teaches the art of using mental
imagery and affirmations to produce miraculous changes in your life. Gawain explains four simple steps to effective visualizations, (what I like to call *imaginings*):

1. Set Your Goal
2. Create a Clear Idea or Picture
3. Focus on it Often
4. Give it Positive Energy

Soon, I began realizing what the problem had been. I had been putting all of my
focus and mental energy on what I *didn't*
want. Strong emotions, whether positive or
negative, have a way of attracting whatever thoughts are attached to them. I had
been attracting more and more misery to
myself by focusing, (with very strong emotion), on my dread and angst.

I began spending time and energy

thinking about the life I wanted to lead, rather than wallowing in discontent. The picture became clearer with each new thought. By journal-writing specific scenes from the life I desired as a well-loved author and speaker teaching wholeness, I reinforced the imaginings. With each written and imagined visualization my heart beat faster in anticipation of dreams-come-true. A sweet knowingness crept into my days.

The key to successful creative imagining is to envision or write it as if it is happening *right now*. Our subconscious mind doesn't know the difference between fact and fiction. This is why this technique is so powerful in creating change in our lives. Getting our imagination working in the *present tense* makes it more believable to our subconscious. And the more believable the vision is, the more excited we become. The more excitement and passion attached to the vision, the quicker it manifests into our lives. But, don't get hung up on a specific time limit, just relax and enjoy the

process of using your imagination in this
way. It really is a lot of fun!

While practicing daily visualizations, I
was struck by the similarities between this
and the Dream Book concept that I had
created years before. I would cut and paste
magazine photos and ad copy to create colorful Dream Books for each of my heart's
desires. The results had been amazing.

One example was the time I desperately desired to own land high in the Rockies. Having no money and no idea how this
could come about, I remembered how
quickly other dreams had materialized
after creating my specific Dream Books.
So, I began cutting beautiful mountain
photos from *Outside, Ski Country* and
Backpacker magazines and soon had created another divine Dream Book. Splashed
across the stunning scenery on the front it
read, (in mismatched ad-type), "Now is the
time to have your Colorado Dream!"

Within 8 months of completing my Colorado Dream Book, I held title to a devas-

tatingly beautiful piece of high country property. The 1.67 acre property was bordered by national forest land, so it might as well have been 167 acres. The towering snow-capped peaks and thundering creek cascading through the middle of the property made it unmistakably the answer to my heart's desire. You see, the land looked strikingly similar to one of the photos in my Dream Book. It was below market, on the market for merely days and, (this is the biggee), *owner* financed. Thank God, no one even checked my credit! Now *that's* a miracle!

You can be sure of the miraculous, creative power of vivid imagining, whether it be by creating a Dream Book, simply meditating on a clear picture of your desire, or by written visualizations. Whatever you can do to create a clear picture of your dream in your mind's eye, just do it!

As with so many dreamers, my life is a testimony to the power of clear focus. Today, I'm so grateful to be living the very life

I had imagined. Delight, gratitude and amazement continue to dominate my existence nowadays. It's clear that the power of focus, harnessed by daily imaginings, is what brought about such immediate and lasting changes.

Are you living the life you've always dreamed of? If not, bring those long-lost dreams back into your consciousness. Use your fondest dreams as a basis for your creative visualizations and Dream Books.

It's the most natural thing in the world to clearly imagine your fondest dreams. Look at small children if you doubt what I'm saying. I remember watching an old interview of a young boy, maybe 7 years old, bubbling out visions of his life as a golf pro. That little dreamer was Tiger Woods. As you probably know, at age 21 Tiger was the youngest-ever winner of The Masters' in 1997. Just another example of the power of imagination. A crystal clear vision in the mind of a little boy, nurtured and supported through the years, had phenomenal power to manifest miracles.

We are all born to dream. But more importantly, we are all born to *live* our dreams. The difference between Tiger and most people is that he *kept* imagining the life of his dreams. He lived each day with the clear focus that had power to gather the energy required to make it reality. Ask your local quantum physicist to explain how this gathering of energy works. All I know is that it *does!*

Therefore, we are the creators of the life we envision. It's just that most people envision mediocrity by holding onto the same old thoughts day after day. But why not choose to create a wonderful life? The choice is yours. Go ahead, ask yourself, "If nothing were impossible, what would my life be like?" Now begin to create the life you envision. ***Simply Imagine.***

3 Simply Simplify

> *...there is no 'right' way to simplify.*
> *It must be a personal journey taken*
> *by one who knows down deep that*
> *it's time to live life in a more direct*
> *and honest fashion.*
>
> —RKM, *Simply Happy*

Once we become focused on the path of our dreams, simplicity becomes a powerful tool to help clear the way. Living simply rids us of spirit-numbing distractions, too much indebtedness and other obstacles on the journey to freedom.

Living the simple life is not about deprivation, but about consciously choosing to live according to our own preferences. It's about having more time, energy and money to live joyfully and authentically.

Learning to say no is one of the quickest ways to simplify your life. Decide right now to streamline your obligations in order to free-up more time and energy for doing and being what and who you want to. Just because someone asks you to be on a committee or invites you to a party doesn't mean that you are obligated to acquiesce. Unless, of course, the committee or party nurtures your authentic self. This is always the key to making decisions that promote your freedom. Begin asking yourself, "Does accepting this invitation support the highest vision of myself?" If the answer is no, then politely bow out, without excuses.

One of the wonderful benefits of living more authentically is that we find ourselves seeking approval less often. Now that we're approving of ourselves from the inside, we spend less time and energy worrying about what others think of us. Usually people honor our choices about as much as we honor them ourselves.

And if you're worried about the world

going to hell in a handbasket because you're not on that committee, remember that the most effective way to change the world is by changing yourself from the inside out. Then, whatever you do become involved in will be from the heart-level— which makes you infinitely more effective than serving out of guilt or obligation.

Another time-saver is to use your answering machine. Most people forget that a phone was designed as a convenience rather than a distraction. I've saved countless hours of wasted time over the past few years with this one minor adjustment in my perception. Rarely do phone calls have to be answered right away. Choose a convenient time every day to return all calls and keep them brief.

All of my friends and most associates know that I prefer talking five minutes or less on the phone. You'd be surprised how much quality communication can take place during a brief phone conversation. If you know someone who rattles on end-

lessly, kindly tell them about your 5-min-
ute policy then give them your undivided
attention. Chances are they will begin seeing the superior benefits of quality-versus-
quantity.

Of course, weekly phone calls to your
mother are an exception to the rule. But,
this too, is much more effective if done
from a heart-level, rather than out of guilt
or obligation. As always, your decisions
and actions should be based on your highest vision. As with all of the suggestions in
this book, use what works for you.

One of the most empowering ways to
simplify is to streamline your spending.
Too many people get sucked into a vicious
cycle of purchasing big-ticket cars, homes
and vacations only to find themselves
working more and more overtime to pay
for these outward appearances of abundance. All the while they are becoming
more and more destitute in spirit as a result of the drudgery of this self-imposed
bondage. They get caught up in mindless

consumerism—buying into the ad campaigns that tell them to be whole and happy they must wear this brand of running shoes or drive that type of sports-utility vehicle.

After more than five years of living simply it has occurred to me: If the product is advertised via national television or magazine ads, you are simply paying too much. Unless, of course, you buy the same shoes or vehicle second-hand, which is a viable alternative to purchasing retail. Thousands of dollars a year can be saved and funneled into the realization of your dreams by simplifying your budget. The following is an excerpt from my book, *Simply Happy:*

> *A few years ago I was heavily in debt... my credit card bills were outrageous, not to mention the obscene amount of interest being charged each month on money I had spent years before. I was discouraged and overwhelmed.*

Two years later I was completely out of debt. During those two years I asked myself again and again, "Will this purchase get me closer to my goal of being debt-free?" If the answer was no, and it usually was, I would then choose to walk away a stronger, freer person.

In addition to curbing your spending, there are countless other ways to simplify. Think of ways to save time, energy and money—all of which can be spent enjoying more freedom.

A wonderful resource for those seeking to simplify is the quarterly journal, *Simple Living*, 2319 North 45th Street Box 149, Seattle, WA 98103. This delightful publication is chock-full of stories about real-life people who have made the plunge toward freedom by practicing voluntary simplicity. For only $16 per year, this subscription will provide you with plenty of practical ideas and inspiration for your journey to simplicity.

Living simply reveals a liberating paradox. We find that the less we have in our lives the more full our lives become. We realize that happiness comes from living authentically—guided by our inner compass—rather than from keeping obligatory, overloaded schedules or from making pretentious, pricey purchases. So begin claiming your freedom today and *Simply Simplify.*

4 Simply Integrate

Living on earth successfully means embracing and integrating our animal (physical), human (emotional and mental), and divine (spiritual) selves. —Shakti Gawain

Becoming free means honoring all aspects of our being: body, mind and spirit. To attempt exceptional growth in one area without the development of the others can create an imbalance that hinders true freedom. Throughout this book you will find a heavy emphasis on spiritual matters. But, please understand the shift from captivity consciousness to freedom consciousness happens more easily when all areas are tended to.

By integrating physical, mental and

spiritual growth, we find wings to fly above our former limiting beliefs. As we nurture all parts of ourselves, we gain more strength and insight with which to face challenges and find joy. Like all of the ideas herein, integration is simple.

Good nutrition, regular exercise and yoga are some simple ways to free the body from ill-health and limitations. As we treat our bodies with more respect, we are amazed at the response: more energy, better shape and increased joy. I remember a time when a debilitating depression overwhelmed me. A wise doctor gave me an unusual, yet life-changing prescription: Eat a balanced diet and exercise at least 20 to 30 minutes a day.

Good nutrition is not about diet pills and crash diets. Eating a balanced diet is as simple as looking on the back of your cereal box to study the Food Guide Pyramid. Follow these straightforward guidelines and watch your body and health respond with better health and higher energy levels. Chances are your mood will even rise. Healthy eating is a natural anti-depressant, as my doctor knew when he wrote that perceptive prescription.

Likewise, regular exercise can elevate and stabilize our moods. Exercise doesn't have to include visits to a health club or a personal trainer. Brisk walking, jogging, running, floor exercises, dancing to your favorite music, jumping rope or calisthenics are some of the simple yet life-changing ways you can integrate good health into your life.

Essential to our body's freedom is the enjoyment of simple sensuous pleasures. Allow yourself to indulge in the delights of sight, sound, smell, touch and taste. So often we numb ourselves to the pleasures of our senses. Worlds of wonder can open up as we begin to honor this aspect of ourselves.

A walk outdoors becomes joyfully intoxicating as fragrances, colors, textures, and sounds remind us how effortlessly delight can flood our soul. Stroking the silky back of a faithful pet; tenderly caressing our beloved; writing in our best penmanship for the sheer joy of it; bellowing out the words of our favorite song turned up full volume on the car stereo; sipping deep red wine from a sparkling crystal goblet or steaming aromatic herbal tea before bedtime; reveling in the wild, windy pleasure of a Harley; slowly savoring the flavors of a gourmet meal; luxuriating in a bath filled with aromatherapy bath salts. All of these reacquaint us with our freedom to enjoy life's simple sensual pleasures. Exercising our senses frees us to enjoy each precious present moment.

The exercise of our brain is equally liberating. Reading, studying, and learning help us to tap into the incredible power of our mind. A wonderful movie that touches on the incomprehensible storehouse in our brain is *Phenomenon* with John Travolta. If you haven't seen this heart-warming, creative masterpiece I strongly urge you to rent the video. It's a look at what might happen if our brain were used fully. This charming movie encourages us to develop more of our unlimited potential.

Exercising our brain is easily done. Each day you have a choice, to starve or stimulate your mind. You can choose to go through life with blinders on, or engage your brain by honoring your inborn curiosity.

Each week, simply by reading one book on something you've always wondered about, you can effortlessly break the stagnating TV habit. Subscribing to a professional journal or newsletter in a science or study that you're interested in not only exercises your brain but can lead to some exciting new options in your life's path. A resource I highly recommend is *The Journal of Noetic Sciences*, 475 Gate Five Road, suite 300, Sausalita, CA 94965. This quarterly journal reports on fascinating research into the mind-body-spirit connection.

And why not enroll in a college course just for the fun of it? Visit the library or your favorite book store at least twice a month and promise yourself to never leave empty-handed. But, like everything else in this book, it's the continued daily practice that leads to phenomenal results. Having a stack of unread books and journals won't lead to the freedom you seek.

Nothing has stimulated my mental growth more than the incorporation of regular reading into my weekly schedule. Rather than always going out with friends to be entertained, I began choosing to spend more evenings developing my mind.

Here's a challenge for you: Why not turn off the TV, resist the temptation to engage in mind-dulling amusements and open an uplifting book? The Suggested Reading section offers some great solutions to your entertainment addiction. The more you develop your intellect, the less you'll crave mindless diversions.

There is nothing wrong with entertainment so long as it doesn't take the place of your own personal development and evolution. Like any other habit, careless entertainment can become a form of bondage that keeps you from growing toward freedom.

The simple truth is: The way you spend your time will either set you free or tighten the bonds that hold you. This doesn't mean you must lead a life void of fun. Choosing to spend a weekend relishing the windy freedom of a Harley, watching an inspiring movie or opera—or countless other nurturing entertainment choices—you can enjoy life without vegetating or damaging your wholeness. Therefore, selectively choose entertainment that inspires and enriches your life.

The development of your spiritual side deserves special mention, so the remainder of the book is about developing this most powerful aspect of your identity.

On your journey to freedom remember to honor all aspects of yourself: body, mind and spirit. Ignoring any of these will result in an imbalance that inhibits your freedom. By living a balanced life, you will begin to realize your unlimited potential for dreams-come-true. So, as you decide how to spend your time each day, remember to *Simply Integrate.*

5   Simply Write

Rules of Journal Writing:
1. Date your entries as you go.
2. Don't make any other rules.
        —Christina Baldwin

Giving credence to your innermost feelings and dreams is one of the most empowering paths to freedom. Regular journal writing is a simple way to do this. A spiritual journal is more than a diary. It's a daring delving into your very soul. A look at the deeper, higher aspects of who you are and where you are headed. Your journal is a place for finding answers. As you weave your way through the questions, answers come with surprising clarity. In your journal, you learn about your freedom to choose.

As you write about the inevitable questions that arise as you begin to live more consciously, you are able to make better choices. You are able to discover who you really are. Able to become more and more true to your unique nature.

It was in the secret passages of my journal that I finally realized I must be true to my longing for solitude. For years I saw this particular aspect of my Self as unacceptable, antisocial, dark behavior. By taking a closer look at my feelings, and the consequences of being untrue to my nature, I was able to come to a life-changing decision. Until I honored my longing for solitude, I would never be truly, completely Rebecca.

I began to understand that there is a higher purpose for all of our deepest desires. I never dreamed that my desire to camp alone in the wilderness would eventually lead to my path as a writer and speaker. How could I have known that the solitude and wonder of the Rockies would inspire me to write and create a curriculum for change?

I began to understand that our dreams and unique desires are our chance to be true to our spiritual nature, the most powerful part of who we are—the part of us that can touch the world in immeasurable ways. And a spiritual journal is one of the best ways to discover those dreams.

A journal is also a place we can talk to God. Oh, you say, you already pray, so why write it down? Well, there's something very inspiring about writing to God on Tuesday for guidance and writing about the perfect answer that arrived by Saturday. You begin to see a pattern: God hears! And God answers! Big prayers. Little prayers. And if you ever begin to doubt... well, you've got undeniable written documentation of all your requests and the subsequent answers.

Nothing builds your faith more than talking to God in your journal. A fun example of this happened recently during one of my retreats. I had taught about journal writing to God on Friday evening. Saturday morning Chelsea asked to read her entry to the group. In her journal, she had asked for guidance about an unhealthy relationship she had just ended. She knew the time had come to get on with her life. All she wanted was some sort of sign that she had made the right decision about breaking up with Donald.

On Sunday morning, as we were enjoying breakfast, Bill, the owner of the retreat center, walked in and handed Chelsea a piece of paper with a doctor's name and number scribbled on it. He said, "Here, Chelsea, you seem to have an admirer." He went on to explain that the doctor had seen Chelsea on a TV news interview that Thursday evening, in which she had mentioned coming to our retreat. The doctor had told Bill how awkward he felt calling, but "something just clicked" and he just had to know if Chelsea was single.

We all whooped with excitement! We didn't know whether or not the doctor was

Mr. Wonderful, but the group did know that this was the sign Chelsea had prayed for. She ended up dating the doctor for a while before deciding how much she enjoyed being alone. But Chelsea knows without a shadow of a doubt, (because she has written proof), that the Sunday morning message was the answer to the Friday evening prayer.

No matter how you choose to use your journal, as a dialogue with yourself, with God, or both... just be sure of its power to shape your dreams. Think of it as your *Life's Companion,* as Christina Baldwin named her book about spiritual journal writing. Baldwin writes about several types of journal exercises.

When teaching journal writing during *Simply Follow Your Bliss* retreats, my two favorite types are: timed entries and flow writing. These are for times you're not sure where to start. Timed entries are usually for 5 minutes and flow writing is simply writing about the first object you see and following your stream of consciousness as you write. Both of these exercises teach you to trust that no matter where you start, words will come. Says Baldwin:

> *Flow writing is the tip of the iceberg, touching on thoughts that ride deeply in your mind.*

It's always great fun to see new journal writers awe-struck at their own depth and creativity. Many an entry has began something like: "Well, here I am on the roof garden overlooking the Pacific in sunny Mexico... supposed to be writing for 5 minutes and I haven't a clue what to write about..." Within the first two or three minutes each participant begins to skim the proverbial iceberg and stands amazed at the insights discovered so effortlessly.

Here are a few journal exercises to get you started. Ask your Highest Self, Inner Child, God—whoever you feel comfortable journaling to—any of the following questions. Be sure to write whatever comes, never editing or stopping until the answers seem complete.

- — What am I at my essence?
- — What is blocking me?
- — Highest Self, what have you learned that I need to know?
- — In what ways have I been giving away my power?
- — How can I begin reclaiming my power again?

It is by asking the right questions that we get the perfect answers. You will be amazed at the insights revealed in the pages of your journal.

Regular journal writing is like regular exercise. Until you try it for yourself, you'll never experience its undeniable benefits. Of all the keys to freedom mentioned in this little book, this is one of the easiest to begin and one of the most empowering.

So, grab a legal pad, a fancy journal book, a spiral notebook. Don't worry about spelling, penmanship or correct grammar.

Write whatever comes to mind, even if it seems trivial. Keep writing for at least two pages. The more you write, the more insights will flow. The form doesn't matter, only the content.

If you're afraid someone will read it, buy a fireproof metal box and hide the box, (and the key). Ask a trusted friend to destroy your journals if anything ever happens to you. Or, better yet, trust the universe that after you're gone things will unfold as they should! There's no good reason not to write, only lame excuses to stay locked in your self-imposed prison of doubt and fear.

Do you want to keep wandering forever lost in the ominous labyrinth of confusion? Or find the elusive passageway to freedom that awaits discovery in the pages of your journal? The choice, as always, is yours. Why not choose to waltz effortlessly into the sunshine of freedom? Why not *Simply Write.*

6   Simply You

*And this above all, to thine
own self be true.*
                    —Shakespeare

On the journey to freedom, it's necessary to be true to your unique nature. You possess talents, experiences and abilities that are unique in all the universe. Your special combination of these can benefit the world in untold ways, not to mention the joy that comes from living authentically. So begin experiencing the freedom of being true to who you are.

If you prefer solitude, don't look for a job in outside sales. If you love people, don't get stuck as a mail order operator. Look for ways to express your individuality through your work and play.

If you love nature and solitude, try a camping trip rather than a cruise. If you love flowers, begin a small garden, even if you live in a high rise. Simply buy some pots, potting soil and seeds and watch yourself bloom right along with your plants. How we spend our time either nurtures or impairs who we are. Start paying attention to how you spend your time each and every day.

But, what if you are so out of touch with your identity that you don't even know what you like to do? Well, that's where journal writing comes in handy. Give yourself permission to delve into your innermost desires in the pages of your *life's companion*. Ask yourself, "If money were no object, who would I be? What would I do?" The truth is: Money shouldn't be an object when it comes to being true to the real you. The best way to begin living authentically is by paying attention to your preferences.

And speaking of authenticity... that's what true freedom is all about. Being authentic. Being real, genuine. How often have we chosen to wear a superficial mask when meeting new people? We try to impress someone with who we are, (or should I say... with who we aren't?), then we wonder why we are so uncomfortable and stressed when we are with those people.

We even let this madness spill over into our appearance. If we have curly hair, we straighten it. Those with straight hair pay top dollar for curls. I've always had wild-looking, unruly hair. For years I tried to tame it by curling, straightening or styling it. Now I spend about 30 seconds on my hair by putting it up in a pony tail or by pulling it up in comb-clip. It's neat, it's simple and, more importantly, it's simply me!

True friendship teaches us about authenticity. We would never consider letting a superficial mask steal the joy from time spent with our best friend. We experience true freedom as we genuinely relate and share with a kindred soul. Besides our own insecurities, there is nothing that keeps us from allowing that freedom to permeate all of our encounters.

The quickest route to being uniquely you is to accept others for who they are. Focus on seeing the goodness in the other person. This automatically shifts you from control to freedom. It is not our responsibility to control others. Not only is it not our responsibility, it is impossible! Oh, sure, we've all known people who seem to be able to control others with guilt or manipulative schemes. But we all know, intuitively, that manipulation is not real power. Real power is found in loving and accepting ourselves and others as we are.

Life becomes much more rewarding when we are able to see the divinity in everyone. Our days become like a treasure hunt with lavish jewels discovered in every encounter. Rather than judging someone for being different, we begin to appreciate their uniqueness and inherent goodness.

And most important to our quest for

freedom is that when we are able to see the goodness in others, we begin to see it in ourselves. This revelation is paramount to our freedom, because freedom is impossible without self-love.

So, next time you are tempted to hide behind a mask, remember: To experience true freedom, just be *Simply You.*

7   Simply Relax

*It's fundamental for expanding plea-
sure that you discover you can exist
almost all the time in a natural state
of effortless enjoyment.*
                    —Harold Bloomfield

We are never really free until we can
completely relax. A deep breath, a long
soak in the a hot bubble bath, lying on a
deserted beach bathed in the sun's golden
rays... these images conjure up memories
of deep relaxation. But to be truly free, we
must learn to relax and experience peace
in any situation.

Relaxation is an experience foreign to
many people. Ever wonder what the world
would be like if everyone were more relaxed? I love the philosophy behind the sim-

ple wooden apparatus called The Happy Massager. The card attached to this little smiley-faced wonder says that the vision of The Happy Massager Corporation is world peace. They figure if everyone felt more relaxed, there would be less fighting in the world.

So, why are we all so tense in the first place? One reason for stress is our need to control others. When we learn that everyone is responsible for their own life and behavior then we are able to relax. Loving people unconditionally, without expectations, allows us to simply relax and enjoy their uniqueness.

But what about when that particular family member or co-worker is getting on your last nerve? First, take a deep breath and remember that we don't *own* someone's "irrational" behavior unless we react to it. Decide to view the situation as an opportunity to exercise your freedom to choose harmony. As we relinquish the need to control, we experience peace. Approach the person with love and acceptance and watch how effortlessly the "problem" is solved.

There are several ways that I have found to relax and experience peace:

— stop judging others so harshly
— stop judging myself so harshly
— walk outside and take three deep breaths
— study a flower, up-close
— walk in the woods
— write in my journal
— listen to soothing instrumental music
— take a long drink of cool water
— feel it washing down to nourish my body
— exercise to good music
— drink herbal tea before bedtime
— practice deep breathing and meditation
— get a massage
— laugh out loud
— cuddle my cats

If fact, animals deserve special mention when it comes to relaxation. The unconditional love of a special animal does more to relax us than just about anything. Watching their playful antics and simple delights has a soothing effect on us after a stressful day at work. Even research has shown that people with pets are more emotionally healthy than those without. Perhaps because animals meet us on a soul-level, unencumbered by ego-walls.

If you haven't yet discovered the joy of loving a furry companion, take a trip to the animal shelter or look in the want-ads. There are plenty of wonderful homeless animals just waiting for someone to call their own. The more you allow that special animal into your heart and home, the more both of you will profit from the relationship. You won't enjoy the same benefits by tying a dog to a post or never allowing a cat on your furniture. Whole-heartedly welcoming an animal into your heart and home can teach you about what's important in life. The happy smile of your dog or the contented purr of the cat will keep you feeling loved and relaxed.

Spending time in nature is another way to rediscover life's simpler joys. The next time you have a few days off, instead of rushing off to a noisy city burgeoning with all forms of entertainment competing for your time, try spending it with nature. Find a quiet cabin or campsite in the woods, a private beach house or an out-of-the-way lodge. Two or three days spent in the rejuvenating presence of nature are worth a month of days off in the city.

Wherever we find harmony, joy and love, we inevitably find peace. And where there's peace, there's freedom. Next time you feel tension, decide to be gentle with yourself and *Simply Relax.*

8 Simply Surrender

> *...in our willingness to step into the
> unknown, the field of all possi-
> bilities, we surrender ourselves to
> the creative mind that orchestrates
> the dance of the universe.*
> —Deepak Chopra

When the idea of surrender first began to
enter my consciousness, I was petrified. I
had spent years trying to gain control. Surrender sounded like giving up. You know,
raising the white flag, losing the war, ad-
mitting defeat. For years I struggled and
forced my way through life. The proverbial
knot in my stomach ever-present, I had
faced life with a suspicious eye and masked
persona.

But through more conscious living I began to notice something. I noticed that the more I struggled, the more I struggled. The concept of surrender began to look more and more appealing. But how does one ever really let go? A couple of years ago I began wondering.

At the time I was a few years into my soul's journey to Self awareness. I found myself facing some financial challenges associated with my new path as a writer and speaker. I wondered if I could ever trust enough to simply surrender.

Then one blessed night my answer came. It was one of those vivid, colorful dreams that seemed to last for hours. The captain of my own small sailing vessel, I was busy preparing a gourmet meal below deck. Very proud of my delicious accomplishment, I offered to feed the crew of a gigantic freighter that pulled up beside me a few hours later.

The captain convulsed in laughter. Condescendingly, she yelled over to me, "You must be joking! How could your tiny vessel

have anything to offer us?" For self-preser-
vation I had to escape her raging ridicule.
Somehow I gunned the motor and sped
away into the dark night.

I found myself speeding into the ominous emptiness of the threatening sea-
scape when I realized I had no idea how to
stop, turn around or even slow down. Suddenly, at about 150 mph, (since I have no
idea what "knots" means), I jerked the
ship into a complete U-turn. Water gushed
in. I was sinking! Just when all seemed
hopeless, I looked out and saw the most
awesome sight.

An astonishing Clydesdale horse stood
upon the water, leisurely lapping up the
liquid beneath him. He turned and looked
deep into my eyes as if to say, "I'm right
here. Don't worry, I'll carry you to safety."
I knew there was nothing to fear.

The next morning, as I wrote about my
moving midnight message, I remembered
an old saying I hadn't heard for years:
When you come to the edge of everything

you know, trust that when you leap... either there will be a net below to catch you, or you will be given wings to fly.

Now I understood! Surrender meant having faith that something—a net, wings, a celestial Clydesdale... *something* would be there to catch me. But until I let go of the struggle, the fear that my "small vessel" had nothing to offer, I could not accept God's perfect answer.

In *The Path to Love*, Deepak Chopra reminds us, *"Surrender is faith that the power of love can accomplish anything, even when you cannot foresee the outcome of a situation."* We are seldom able to spot our Clydesdale waiting patiently on the water. However, as we experience miraculous answers time and again, we begin to feel comfortable with surrender.

Chopra explains how the sometimes gradual process of surrender takes place *"...on every level—physical, mental, and emotional."* He mentions several ways to let go physically. *"...laughter, screaming,*

*shouting, taking a walk, swimming, taking
a long bath, dancing and doing aerobics."*

Of course, the emotional and mental
surrender can come most easily from your
journal writing. As you write about what
troubles you most, a sweet sense of release
bubbles up. In fact, some of my greatest
belly-laughs have come from looking back
through my journal. What a joy to look at
last week's trauma through the accepting
eyes of surrender. The shift in perception
allows us to take a lighter look at life's
twists and turns.

When we surrender, a feeling of wonder replaces the need to control. The re-
sulting joy and peace are enough to keep
us detached. No amount of "successful
manipulation" can replace the peace found
in surrender. Through the practice of surrender we discover that God is supporting
us and our dreams.

The weeks following my Clydesdale
dream, I began to let go of worry. Now that
I was able to enjoy each present moment, a

splendid synchronicity began to permeate my days. Opportunity after opportunity presented themselves as I surrendered my way into the "leap off the edge" of everything I knew. And just as I had expected, I was given wings to fly.

So, if you're tired of losing the present while worrying about the future, it's time to consider the alternative. The freedom found in surrender can only be experienced by a heart who's ready to leap into *now*. If you're ready to fly, ***Simply Surrender.***

9   Simply Renew

The renewing of the mind is a scientific act.... Instead of the old concepts of disease and failure, we are to inject those of liberty, freedom, health, harmony and success.
—Ernest Holmes

Everything. E-V-E-R-Y-T-H-I-N-G begins in our mind first, then manifests into our physical existence. Bad or good. If our mind is full of fear, doubt, lack and limitation—then that is what we experience in our lives. On the other hand, if our mind is filled with gratitude and grand expectations, we will experience the miraculous effects of such thinking.

In *The Science of Mind,* Ernest Holmes writes about the power we possess in our minds:

All thought is creative, according to the nature, impulse, emotion or conviction behind the thought. Thought creates a mold in the Subjective, in which the idea is accepted and poured, and sets power in motion in accordance with the thought.

Think of examples of this truth in your own life. How about the time your mind was full of the possibility of getting that new job... of course you got it! Your mind was convinced of the possibility of finding that special someone... and you did! Your mind was overflowing with excitement about learning how to meditate... and you received a flyer about an affordable retreat teaching meditation techniques.

God always says yes to whatever we believe. Christ taught us that as we believe, so it is done unto us.

But remember, this Universal Truth works both ways. Consider when your mind is full of fear about having a wreck... and you have one. When your mind is plagued

with doubt about getting that promotion...
and you are passed over. Your mind is full
of cynicism about people... which is re-
flected in your disappointing relationships.

The key word is *full*. We all have fleet-
ing negative, fearful thoughts on occasion.
But it is when our minds are *full* of fear,
doubt and negativity that our lives will
manifest misery.

By the same token, when our consciousness is overflowing with possibility, love
and goodness, our outward life begins to reflect the inevitable *miraculous* results. So,
how do we keep our minds filled with goodness rather than fear, doubt and confusion?

By remembering and applying this
truth: What you focus on... you get more of.
And, unfortunately, most people focus on
bad things... by worrying about the very
thing they don't want. Worry puts focus on
the exact opposite of our desired result.

So, how do you put your focus on what
you want? Paul admonishes us: *"...be ye
transformed by the renewing of your mind."*

Just how, you ask, am I going to renew my mind? By filling your mind with goodness.

Continued practice of the suggestions in this book; engaging in random acts of kindness; looking for the good in life and people... these are ways to fill your mind with goodness. Renewing your consciousness is as simple as making better choices about how you spend your time.

Read a life-enhancing book rather than watch a mind-numbing sit-com or soap opera. Listen to a motivational tape or an inspiring concerto while driving rather than the chitter chatter or same old songs on the radio. And don't forget the power you have to create your dreams through creative imagining. Review the *Simply Imagine* chapter for a refresher on this empowering practice.

It's your choice. Claim your freedom by focusing your thoughts on the life you want to lead. Get rid of limiting beliefs, negative thoughts and stagnation by choosing a better way. Every hour of every day, choose to *Simply Renew.*

10 Simply Notice

When someone holds up a flower and shows it to you, he wants you to see it. If you keep thinking, you miss the flower.
— Thich Nhat Hanh

On a particularly overcast Spring morning I began my usual 30-minute walk. Almost immediately I began to notice the irritating slip-and-slide of my wristwatch. Deciding to ignore it, I continued walking. Within a couple of minutes a rash-like redness encircled my wrist. I took the culprit off and slipped it into my pocket.

Suddenly I noticed a brilliant sunburst in the otherwise cloud-filled sky. The dazzling rays created a perfect silver lining around the ominous cloud. Revelation burst into my awareness like lifting the lid of a chest brimming with priceless treasure. It was as if God was saying, "Stop watching the time and notice this Heaven!"

The remainder of that walk was spent in wonder. Reveling in the preciousness of our universe, I noticed what so often had been ignored: the colorful contrast of spring-green treetops against the smoky, gray-dark sky; daffodil trumpets, perched skyward... blasting out, "Notice me!" in unison; the personalities of the pansies dancing in the breeze; the gentle gurgling of our cascading creek; the snow-white blooms of Dogwoods; the intoxicating fragrance of soggy springtime soil. I just couldn't stop noticing!

How often had these delicious delights gone unappreciated? Even the weeds spoke to my heart. Their bright-white, royal-purple and luminous yellow blooms seemed there to remind me of Barry Neil Kaufman's wisdom:

> *The only difference between a flower and a weed is a judgment.*

And so, I found another key to freedom that blissful morning: the freedom found in present moment awareness. By truly being in the present moment, we are free from worry about the past or future. Free to notice and relish the enchantment that surrounds us continually.

Since that diamond day, my walks have been less about physical fitness and more about spiritual exercise. A few weeks after that morning I was reading *Peace is Every Step* by Thich Nhat Hanh and was touched by a poem he included which was written by a friend of his who had died at age 28. As the young man was walking on a particular morning, he was struck by the sight of a dahlia, stopped and wrote this poem:

> *Standing quietly by the fence,*
> *you smile your wondrous smile.*
> *I am speechless, and my senses are filled*
> *by the sounds of your beautiful song,*
> *beginningless and endless.*
> *I bow deeply to you.*

I wept as I remembered the morning of my

special revelation, so thankful that I had not died at the tender age of 28. For it took nearly 40 years for me to realize the freedom found in seeing, really *seeing* a flower by the fence.

And how often do we miss the endearing little qualities of the those loved ones that we often take for granted? Instead of raging on about their shortcomings, let's start to notice the enchanting mannerisms that we often forget.

Being a spontaneous, "fly by the seat of my pants" kind of person, my marriage to Karl has often been a challenge. His need for order and attention to detail I found perplexing and sometimes irritating. Until I started to notice that he brought that same diligence into the care of our cats. I have a delightful photo that sits on my desk of him gingerly picking off flea carcasses from a flea-bath-soaked, sprawled-legged, exhausted kitty. Every time I look at it, I see Karl's divinity. His trademark persnickitiness has transformed to a charming quirk that I've come to adore.

Claim your freedom today. Notice the wonders all around you. The flowers, the rustling leaves, the silver-linings, the spontaneity of a child, the endearing traits of your loved ones... each a testament to life's preciousness. They are all there especially for you. Just waiting for you to *Simply Notice.*

11   Simply Feel

*If the choice feels comfortable, I
will plunge ahead with abandon.
If the choice feels uncomfortable,
I will pause and see the consequences of my action with my
inner vision.* —Deepak Chopra

A direct path to freedom is through honoring our feelings. That's why regular journal
writing is so powerful. As we begin to take a
closer look at the fabric of our lives, we can
no longer ignore the texture of our feelings.
We begin to understand that our feeling
about something is our truth about it.

Sadly, more often than not, we choose
to analyze our feelings rather than honor
them. And soon the feelings are shoved
down deep which leads to frustration and

captivity consciousness. Unexpressed feelings come back to haunt us in ugly ways.
Here are a few ways that blocked feelings
might manifest themselves in our lives:

— illness	— irritation
— depression	— judgment
— neurosis	— rage
— poor relationships	— fear

Again, journaling is a very effective outlet
for processing previously unexpressed emotions.

There is a well-spring of joy within
each of us. Look at any baby and you'll get
the picture. Any baby whose needs have
been met is bubbling with bliss. We were
born to be happy. So what happens to this
well-spring of joy over the years? It becomes dammed-up with those unexpressed
emotions. Learning to process these feelings ultimately unblocks us. The bliss that
we were born with returns as the blocks
are cleared.

Processing feelings is most effective if

you do it as they come up, (rather than years later in therapy). This entire book is about shifting from victim to co-creator. Paying attention to how you feel about something will put you in touch with your inner guidance. Following that guidance hastens the fulfillment of our dreams.

People who continue to trudge through life ignoring their feelings are the ones who remain bound, locked inside the prison of buried emotions and analytical responses. Rather than paying attention to that impulse to take a creative writing class, (which could quite possibly lead to an exciting new path), you opt to analyze the dangers of following your heart. The result: You remain locked in a "safe" job that leaves you uninspired and depressed, feeling like a victim. Gloria Steimen, in her 1992 bestseller *Revolution from Within* tells us:

> *Each of us has an inner compass that helps us know where to go and what to do. Its signals are interest, excitement,*

*the joy of understanding for its own
sake, and the sort of fear that is a sign
of being in new territory—and therefore of growth.*

So the next time you get the urge to go
on a camping trip out West, take time to
check your inner compass. Notice the excitement—the new interest in outdoor
equipment catalogs—the fear of being in
new territory—the empowerment of new
growth. Then do yourself a life-changing
favor and resist the analytical urge to talk
yourself out of it. Just honor your feelings,
your excitement, your interest. Just do it!

As you begin honoring your feelings
your life takes on a sparkling vibrancy that
you thought you'd left back in childhood.
Imagine living life in wonder, as if each
new day was truly a *new* day. What if you
began right now? What if the excitement
you feel right now as you think of taking
that class, traveling to that new place,
starting that new project—what if you
honored that excitement by stepping into

that dream rather than remaining in your *safe* rut of mediocrity?

Think of it. It's *safer* to stay in prison. Three squares a day. Guards to monitor your every move. No money worries. No decisions to make. Just mundane safety. And the comfort of knowing exactly where you'll be tomorrow. All of this safety is yours by simply continuing to ignore your feelings. Yes, it does sound ridiculous. Yet, doesn't it sound eerily familiar?

But, what if it's been so long since you honored your feelings that you honestly don't know how? Well, try this simple exercise. First, make a list of decisions you want to make. Notice I said *want* not need. We are honoring feelings here, not shoulds.

Now, take each one and ask yourself, What are my feelings about this? For instance, if you write down that you want to decide about taking a class in anthropology at the local university, ask yourself what are my feelings about this?

Now wait a few moments and notice. Do

your feelings indicate excitement or dread? If your overall feelings are that of interest and joy, then a liberating decision would be to take the class as soon as possible. If, on the other hand, you find that the thought of taking the class causes feelings of dread and fatigue, then you will hopefully decide against it.

But what if you feel both excited and fearful? Well, excitement is the key feeling. Excitement is the *inner compass* pointing our way to freedom. But what about that fear? Lots of times the fear is a result of stepping out of our comfort zone. The fearful ego part of us never likes stepping into uncharted territory. Ego would rather stay locked in a safe prison than ever try anything new.

It's your choice, captivity or freedom. So, as psychologist Susan Jeffers says, *"Feel the fear and do it anyway."* The first step is always the scariest. As you face and conquer your fear of the unknown a new sense of power arises within you. You begin to get a glimpse of your limitless potential.

Nothing takes the joy out of life more than trying to analyze the outcome of every decision. I remember the guilt I suffered about leaving my students when I decided to quit teaching. I worried that my decision to leave would be bad for them. One of my favorite groups of students would be seniors the following year, and many asked if I wouldn't mind staying just one more year until they had graduated. I decided to leave at the end of their junior year to follow my dream, and wondered about the outcome.

In the years that have followed I've received several letters, visits and calls from my students. Many have mentioned how inspired they were by my courage to follow a dream. Recently I ran into two of them in a second-hand clothing store. They hid under the racks and jumped out to surprise me. After the laughter died down, Derek and Lester went on to say that they remembered the day in our support group when we were sharing our dreams for the future. They reminded me that mine was to become a writer and to spend each summer in the mountains.

These two inspiring young men shared with me how happy they were to know someone who had realized her dream, because they were on the way to realizing their own dream. The two talented musicians said that my life had inspired them to keep moving in the direction of their dream. As a result their rock and roll band was experiencing some exciting successes.

If you want to stay stuck, keep worrying about the future. Keep trying to second-guess each decision you make. Analyzing the reasons why you cannot follow your feelings will disempower and discourage you. So, why not simply honor your feelings?

Kim, a 39 year old single mother of two teenagers, attended one of my *Simply Follow Your Bliss* retreats in Yelapa, Mexico. When we came to the exercise mentioned above, the decision was about whether or not to follow the urge to sell her delicious poppyseed bread to the public. When she came to the part of monitoring her feelings, she felt a surge of empowering energy that carried her to the eventual opening of *Ms. Poppy's Baked Goods*. If you've ever had the pleasure of sinking your teeth into Kim's famous mouth-watering sweet bread, you surely understand the delicious benefits of paying attention to the inner compass.

I challenge you, the next time you have strong feelings about something, set yourself free to follow their lead. Trust in the goodness of life and know that your feelings are a sign pointing the way to your bliss. The next time, don't analyze them away, *Simply Feel.*

12 Simply Conscious

Consciousness is not a destination at which we finally arrive. It is an ongoing, ever-deepening, infinitely expanding process...
—Shakti Gawain

One morning, as I walked down to our creek to begin a 30-minute run, my mind was filled with what I'd just read in Neale Donald Walsh's *Conversations with God:*

The most rapid way to change a root thought... is to reverse the thought-word-deed process... Do the deed that you want to have the new thought about.

Delighted at the wise choice to *do the deed* of getting back in shape, I began slowly running laps. It had been several months since I'd run and atrophy threatened my muscles and stamina. The new thought was a healthier, shapelier me. The deed: My morning runs of the past few days.

The first time around, I stumbled over something, caught myself just before falling, and went on without another thought of it. Second time around, I tripped in the same spot. It became clear that an important lesson was unfolding right before my eyes. The third time around, I spotted the problem—a huge walnut—and simply ran around it. The next time around I scooped up the potential hazard and tossed it safely into the woods.

The message was so clear. Even though I had been learning powerful new techniques for change, I needed to wake up! All the knowledge in the universe couldn't keep me from stumbling if I refused to become aware of the *now*. Sure, the technique of *doing the deed first* would enhance and even change my life, but I needed to become fully conscious of the priceless gifts of each present moment.

In *The Path of Transformation*, Shakti Gawain explains:

Making a commitment to your consciousness growth means making a decision to become aware of and understand as much as you can about yourself, others, life, and the universe. It involves looking at life as a learning experience in which every single thing that happens to us can be seen as a potential gift to help us develop our full potential.

By living consciously, we avoid stumbling. Unconscious living causes stagnation, repeated errors and captivity. By living more consciously we open ourselves up to growth, wiser choices and freedom. Simply by paying attention, we begin to see a very different world. We begin to understand that we live in a benevolent universe that leans forward to bless us as we are able to receive.

In his phenomenal bestseller, *Celestine Prophecy*, James Redfield speaks of:

...the process of consciously evolving yourself, of staying alert to every coincidence, every answer the universe provides for you.

One of my goals for each *Simply Follow Your Bliss* retreat is to teach the value of living more consciously. We begin slowly awakening to our inner power by becoming more and more conscious through simple individual or group exercises.

As the week progresses the *Bliss* participants have gained enough spiritual confidence to practice being conscious of God's guidance through journal writing. You, too, will want to try this enlightening exercise. Begin by taking some relaxing, deep breaths to center yourself. Then write, "OK, God, what do you want me to do?" No matter what images or thoughts come, write. Write everything, never censoring. As you let go of expectations and ego, insights will come. Following is an excerpt from one such entry. As I sat on *Casa Milagros'* breezy roof garden, basking in the

sunshine of this pristine Mexican paradise, the guidance flowed effortlessly onto
the pages:

OK, God, what do you want me to do?

*Relax. Breathe deeply. Listen. Look.
See. Really See. Flow. Float. Learn
from the soaring birds—how they effortlessly glide higher and higher. A
slight dip of a wing guides them to new
heights. Like your focus... a powerful
force in your new journey of effortless
success, joy and peace.*

*See me in the sun-drenched blue
bucket, the sparkling diamonds on the
water and my painted sky. In Mary's
foot on the wall, Tom's innocent brilliance and Nanette's honest opening.
Hear me in windsong of the palms. Pay
attention to every rooster's crow, every
birdsong, motor boat, smiling face.
Every sip of hot tea, every delicious bite
of life. Know that it's all Me. All a reminder of my love for you.*

Know that you are able, because

you are Me. You are completely safe and completely loved. You have done well to teach the value of Silence—of listening to my voice, of paying attention to me each and every moment of each and every hour of each and every day.

How else could the birds fly? How else could the fish swim—easily and effortlessly. They have no ego walls to filter my voice. So if you want to fly easily and effortlessly into your bliss, be still and know that I AM God. Be still and know that I am you! Be still, my child, be still. And know that I am joy. I am hope. I am peace. I am Kim's poppyseed bread, Lynn's sweet hugs and Melissa's unbridled waterjoy. I am every chapter of every book you write. I am bliss. I am you and we've only just begun to live.

Spread your wings and fly higher and higher in joy, peace and love. And know, my child, that you never left the garden.

Every time you practice the "OK, God..." exercise, you will be amazed at the love and answers that flow effortlessly from within. You will know that the words are universal and true. As Neale Donald Walsch reminds us in *Conversations with God,* Spirit talks to everyone. All the time. The question is not to whom God talks, but who listens.

Waking up to the intelligence and guidance of the universe expands our capacity for freedom and joy. We understand that there are no small things, no meaningless incidents.

So, if you want to experience the freedom of a life filled with meaning, consider awakening to become *Simply Conscious.*

13   Simply Accept

When you struggle against this moment, you're actually struggling against the entire universe... Know that this moment is as it should be.   —Deepak Chopra

Freedom is about experiencing peace, no matter what circumstances we find ourselves in. But what about when our heart is breaking? What about when we lose a loved one or blow a big deal? How can we experience peace in the midst of a crisis?

Well, first of all, let me tell you: This is the second time I've written this chapter. The first time, I began differently. Less empathetically. That was three days ago. I had decided to complete this book within six weeks in order to get it to the publisher before the upcoming retreat in Mexico. After I completed the eleventh chapter, my computer crashed.

Now this little computer glitch would not have been a tragedy had I followed my inner guidance, which for several days had urged me to print out my work. "No," ego kept saying, "wait until you've edited some more. What if someone saw the mess it's in now?" So, for eleven chapters, I had failed not only to print out my work, but also to make a back up copy on the hard drive. Having never experienced a computer crash before, the idea of making backup copies never occurred to me.

I tried everything to retrieve it. After several hours, numerous phone calls, and countless failed attempts, I began to cry. Wail would be a better word. I can't remember the last time I cried that hard. I had tried to recall even one sentence of the missing manuscript and was completely blank. I couldn't even recollect the titles of all the chapters!

To make matters worse, I kept beating myself up for not following my intuition and printing it. How could I have been such an idiot? In the midst of my hell, the still small voice had a revealing message: "Remember your last sentence."

I didn't have to think long to remember what I had written just before the crash:

> *Rather than judge a situation as bad, we must realize that everything that "happens to us" leads to our highest good.*

I couldn't help but chuckle, tears still streaming down. A sweet peace enveloped me. I knew everything would not only be OK, it would turn out wonderfully. Somehow this "tragedy" would turn to triumph.

And that's all it took. A simple change in perception caused me to accept the situation as is, rather than writhing in the pain of my judgment.

I was so excited about this insight, I ran upstairs to write in my journal. On impulse I grabbed the book lying next to it, *Conversations with God*. It fell open to this passage:

> *Pain results from a judgment you have made about a thing. Remove the judgment and the pain disappears.*

I couldn't believe my eyes! Not only had my inner voice spoken clearly, now the words of Neale Donald Walsch's inspired work jumped off the page to reaffirm God's message. There was no way I could remain in sorrow. I realized it was completely my choice. I could remain in the hell of my past perception or I could bask in the light of heaven as I let go of judgment.

I remembered Christ's message: *"The kingdom of heaven is within."* At that moment I knew that within me was the power to choose heaven by seeing with a new perception. I lost eleven chapters because, somehow, the experience was leading me to the highest good.

As I write this chapter I haven't the

foggiest idea how, or even *if*, the original eleven will be retrieved. But I do know that I have found the peace of acceptance and trust that whatever comes of this *tragedy* will be for the highest good.

Learning to suspend judgment is the direct route to freedom... from guilt, pain, and hopelessness. Through acceptance our lives become full of meaning and purpose. Rather than experiencing life as a victim of capricious circumstances, we are able to bask in the comfort of knowing that there are no coincidences. There are no mistakes.

So the next time you are experiencing the hell of judgment, decide instead to experience the peace of heaven—*Simply Accept.*

14 Simply Grateful

*The power of gratefulness
caught me by surprise.*
—Sarah Ban Breathnach

Several years ago Karl and I lived in a tiny house packed tightly between two other matchbox dwellings. This was all our finances, (and consciousness), would afford us at the time. We only had one tree. Well, actually, it was the neighbor's tree, but it hung over our back fence. So, I claimed it as mine.

The only way to get to this little gem of nature was between our old shed and Mary's garden. It was a cramped area, only three feet wide. I remember dragging my lawn chair into that tiny space and climbing awkwardly into my hidden haven.

Reveling in the simple solitude, I would write in my journal and gaze up at that little apple tree. Gratitude overcame me every time I sat under its comforting limbs, so thankful to enjoy this patch of paradise amidst clapboard and cement.

Nowadays, I'm able to spend each summer high in the Rocky Mountains surrounded by the wonders of nature. The remainder of the year I live in a cottage in the woods by a creek. The towering timbers remind me of the multiplying power of genuine gratitude. I am convinced that my sincere gratefulness for that little fruit tree is what has allowed an even greater abundance of nature to flow into my life. God delights in giving to those who ardently appreciate the gifts.

In addition to the multiplying effects, there are other inherent benefits of a grateful heart. Gratitude keeps us focused on the good in our lives. The next time you find yourself moaning about some less than perfect aspect of your life, try practicing a little gratitude. The old hymn "Count Your Blessings" is a reminder to turn from lamentation to appreciation.

The next time you are discouraged about some aspect of your life, try looking for specific ways you are blessed in that area. For instance, if you are experiencing financial challenges, look for ways abundance is already flowing into your life. Money is nothing but an outpicturing of what you hold in your consciousness. If you harbor thoughts of lack and limitation, that's what your financial experience will manifest as.

Gratitude helps us to realize how very rich we are. By keeping our mind on what's right, more goodness flows into our lives. Remember you get more of what you focus on. Good or bad. A grateful heart keeps our consciousness full of the awareness that we live in an abundant universe.

Think of how many times people have brought gifts into your life. Not only material gifts, but treasures of encouragement, faith, acceptance and love.

Why not express your gratitude to these special souls? Make a habit of writing one sincere Thank You card at least once a month. Think back to a special teacher, a distant friend or relative whose kindness still lingers in your heart. Play detective and find those absent angels whose blessings remain.

Nothing feels better than expressing heart-felt thanks. I keep a luscious little supply of artistic blank note cards. Imagining the joy of the delightfully surprised recipient transforms the monthly task into a special blessing. As the card fills up with gratitude, my heart fills up with happiness.

Perhaps the best effect of gratitude is the inner peace it brings. As we begin to really notice and appreciate life's gifts, a sweet peace floods our soul. A grateful heart is a heart at peace. And peace is a hallmark of true freedom.

So, on your journey to freedom, may you discover sweet serenity by taking the time to be *Simply Grateful.*

15   Simply Listen

If you cannot hear the Voice for God, it is because you do not choose to listen.

—*A Course In Miracles*

As we progress along the path of freedom, we are reminded again and again of the wisdom of listening to the inner voice. Important insights and liberating perception-shifts are gained as we pay attention to the still small voice within.

But what if you don't "hear voices"? Well, when was the last time you tried to quiet your mind? Think about it.

We all hear voices! All of the time! So, how on earth can you distinguish between the inner voice and all those other raging voices? Well, there are some simple yet telling characteristics of the inner voice.

However, to recognize the inner voice, it's best to describe the ego voice first. The ego voice is loud, insisting, judgmental and always concerned with what others will think. Ego voices come from a place of fear. The attitude of the ego is Me Against Them. Don't listen to that voice! It will cause you to walk around in fear all the time. Fear is disempowering. Fear breeds captivity consciousness.

The inner voice is very different indeed. Quiet and succinct, it will never argue with you. "You are free!" and "Simplify." Such are the life-changing messages of this inner guide. The inner voice comes from a place of love and Oneness. Listen to this voice. It will set you free!

As I shared the wisdom of listening to our inner guidance during a keynote speech, a woman raised her hand and said, "My inner voice must be talking to someone else!" The audience and I chimed with an empathetic chuckle. A lot of people feel this way. "You know, in some cases it's not a voice," I explained, "Maybe it's more like a gut feeling, or an intuitive thought that you somehow know is right." She acknowledged the presence of such feelings of knowingness. I assured her that paying attention to those hunches would lead to an awareness of the inner guidance that's always available to us.

It might be as simple as, "Turn right here." If you heed the message you might avoid an accident or discover a treasure that you would have missed had you taken the normal route home. You might hear, "Hug her." But so often we let the loud insistence of the ego voice convince us. "Don't hug her. She'll think you're crazy! What if she pushes you away? Besides, she'll start expecting you to listen to her problems. You don't have time for all that." And so we miss another golden opportunity to find meaning and joy by following our inner guidance.

I remember one time when the inner guidance showed up in a dream. It was early June. Arriving in Boston for interviews and booksignings for *Simply Happy*, I found myself both excited and fearful about my new path as an author and speaker. Excited about the opportunities to share the healing message of simple happiness, yet fearful about the lack of certainty in my future. As a high school teacher I had always known what to do and where I would be tomorrow, next month, next year.

Two nights before my last appearance I had a vivid dream. Sitting at the teaching podium in my old classroom, I was visiting with Jay after school. After our conversation, he turned to leave. Before walking out the door, he turned around, looked deep into my eyes and said, "Ms. Merriman, you're coming back for our graduation, aren't you?"

"I wouldn't miss it for the world, Jay!" I woke up with the words still in my head.

Tears welled up as I remembered my conversation with Jay almost one year earlier. Jay's class had been one of my favorite groups of students and we all wished I could have stayed for their senior year. I assured them I wouldn't forget them on their special day. Now, somehow Jay had traveled on the wind to remind me of a promise I'd almost forgotten.

Here I was in Boston on Thursday morning, with two more days of appearances scheduled, and the graduation was Saturday morning in Clarksville, Tennessee. It wouldn't have been any big deal had I flown to Boston, but in order to see some friends along the way, I had driven all the way up the East coast.

By 10:00 P.M. that evening, after a busy day of appearances, I had packed my bags, called and canceled my Friday appointment, and was beginning the longest nonstop drive of my life. I drove straight through, 21 hours. Prayer, excitement and a noble sense of purpose kept me awake. That and a lot of caffeine.

Exhaustion is too mild a word for what my body felt by the time I pulled into the driveway Friday evening. But I fell asleep that night knowing that the coming re-union would be worth it all.

Making it back to that graduation was one of the best decisions I've ever made. The skrieks of excitement and tears of joy made the long drive a distant memory, like a new mother forgetting the pain as she holds her little angel for the first time.

When I finally found Jay, I burst into tears. "Jay, you're the reason I'm here!"

Before I could tell him why, he jumped in, "Ms. Merriman, I had a dream about you the other night!"

After comparing notes, we realized not only did Jay and I appear in each other's dreams the same night... it was the same dream!

Nearly a year later I received a letter from Jay. With his permission, I'm including part of the original letter here. Think of it as a testimony to the wisdom of following our inner guidance, no matter what the cost.

...I miss the good times we all had together in your class. I remember the way you brought out the best in us. You brought our chests out and our heads high with the crazy things you did.... We were proud of you and we all loved you very much... you have touched so many lives and have done so much for people. You can't even imagine how much you have changed many of our lives.

The thing I remember the most is the dream you and I both had... you were at the little thing you had at the front of the class and the final day of my Jr. year I was walking out thinking of what next year might bring and you were thinking of what your new life was going to turn out to be. We both were scared and excited. But as I turn away from you and start to the door I look back and ask, "Ms. Merriman are you going to come see us graduate next year?" and you say "I wouldn't miss it for the world, Jay."

And those words lingered in my head that night till graduation morning. I was upset because I thought you forgot me and your promise. You remember what happened after that... long hours with no sleep.... That morning I was thinking of you so strongly and I could sense something was complete. I walked in and someone told me you were here and I was so glad.... I couldn't believe it. And the next thing I know, here you come crying like a baby. And telling me your dream and I telling you mine. We were freaked out at first but we knew it wasn't an accident you were there.

The next thing I remember I was walking down the line, with my head held high and my chest out—just like in your class, and as I stand there wondering what my future had in store for me I looked up and saw you in the stands. I smiled and thought it was going to be OK. As I walked back and sat down I thought, "That's it, its over! My life as I know it is over." As I look up again I saw you standing there and it hit me. I know how you felt the day when you left—you thought your life was over but all it was is a new chapter opening up. I sat there remembering all of the good times we had and looked up with a tear in my eye.

I knew you were doing the right thing, and I said, "Thank you, Ms. Merriman for giving me my future and for giving me your all."

My students have always amazed me with their gratitude and love. Had it not been my inner voice that urged me to seek another path, I could have never left them. Often, during that first year away from the classroom, I missed them terribly and wondered if I had made the right decision. Jay's letter was like a special delivery from an angel, giving me permission to go wherever my dreams would lead me. I knew the lessons we'd taught each other would last a lifetime.

Your inner guidance may be in the form of a "still small voice," a hunch, or a dream. However it comes to you doesn't matter. What matters is the message.

Try an experiment this week. Quiet the ego voices. Every time you get an idea or hunch that feels right, ignore the protests of ego. Go ahead and follow those inspired feelings. The reward will be peace and an empowering sense of Oneness. The next time the inner voice quietly speaks, ***Simply Listen.***

16   Simply Spirit

*Your true Self, which is your spirit,
your soul, is completely free.*
                    —Deepak Chopra

The more we nurture our inherent spiritual nature, the more real freedom we access. We learn that all of the creative powers of the universe are at our disposal. A rich and meaningful life is ours for the taking.

So often we find ourselves shoving matters of spirit onto the back burner. Yet when a problem presents itself, we intuitively turn to God for answers. Answered prayers and the peace found during these times of spiritual awakening cause us to consider what it might be like to live in Spirit on a daily basis. Rather than continue the roller coaster ride into *sometime spirituality*, we begin to long for a deeper, more meaningful relationship with God and our Higher Self. Ernest Holmes put it well:

> *How we long for a return of that simple trust in life which children have; in their minds there are no doubts—they have not yet been told that they are sinners, destitute of divine guidance and spiritual life.*

For many years I looked outside of myself for happiness, solutions, even salvation. Through my focus on outward reality, my spirit had seemingly starved half to death from lack of nourishment. But through the care of my soul, I have found the truth in Christ's words: *"The kingdom of heaven is within."* Through the focus on my Spiritual Self, I have learned that, truly, heaven is within.

So, how, in a world of deadlines and commitments, can we consistently nourish our spirit? This chapter is dedicated to answering this loaded question. Let's look at some simple ways to nourish this most essential part of us, so that we may reap the benefits of *practical spirituality*—the kind that can bring meaning and freedom to your day-to-day life.

In the first chapter, I mentioned rising one hour earlier each morning. If you don't pay attention to anything else in this book, please know the power made accessible to you through an early hour spent on the care of your soul. Anyone who has consistently tried it has discovered that the hour spent on Spirit is much more invigorating and empowering than one more hour of sleep.

So, what do you do for an entire hour? First of all, look at this hour as your own priceless treasure of solitude. Chances are, if you're up an hour earlier than usual, the house is blissfully quiet. You will come to savor this solitude more than you can imagine. Decide to make this hour uniquely yours by brewing a pot of herbal tea, some gourmet coffee, or whatever booster beverage you would enjoy. If you begin by pampering your physical body, it won't be so resistant to rising early each morning.

Have a special place for your quiet time. If weather and daylight allow, I plop down two old sofa pillows onto the front porch step and savor the morning as I feed my spirit. You might want to create a comfortable corner in your living room or den. Wherever you are, settle into the luxury of this nourishment your soul has been longing for.

I begin by writing whatever is on my mind in the secret pages of my *life's companion*. After I've cleared my mind, I'm able to talk with God, or meditate for about 20 minutes. A good book to read is *How to Meditate* by Lawrence LeShan. This might be one of your early morning readings.

My morning ritual varies, but always begins with journal writing. The remainder of the hour might include:

— reading a spiritual book, (see Suggested Readings)
— listening to the symphony of birdsong
— deep breathing and meditation
— prayer and praise
— outdoor walking meditation

At first, your body might resist rising for your quiet time. But soon you will notice a profound clarity filling the remainder of the day. Soon you wouldn't think of beginning a day without your precious quiet time.

Creativity is a splendid way to tap into your spiritual self. The *Artist's Way* by Julia Cameron is an enlightening work with simple, empowering lessons for developing creativity. As Cameron puts it:

When we open ourselves to exploring our creativity, we open ourselves to God.

Practicing Cameron's lessons either during your morning quiet time or in the evening will draw you closer to your real Self and your God.

Even during periods of great spiritual growth, there may be times that you feel bogged down because of ego voices. In *Your Sacred Self*, Wayne Dyer writes about the part of us that wrestles against spiritual awareness.

> *Ego is your false self... Ego teaches separateness... unable to see ourselves connected to God... our anxiety mounts and our sense of aloneness drives us to seek outer connectedness.*

A Course In Miracles simply states our confusion:

> *We think that without the ego, all would be chaos, the opposite is true. Without the ego, all would be love.*

It is through the daily nourishing of our spirit that we begin to see clearly the freedom found in loving everything and everyone.

As we become more centered, we find ourselves less reactive to people and circumstances. We begin to suspect a higher reason for all encounters and events. Our days blossom into meaningful, often miraculous demonstrations of love and light. The difficult person at work becomes our opportunity to practice the healing power of unconditional love and acceptance. Even rush-hour traffic becomes an opportunity for spiritual exercise. Rather than mumbling obscenities at the person who cuts us off, we find ourselves sending peace to a brother who's obviously feeling none.

As we experience life from our renewed spiritual perception, we begin to experience the Oneness of creation. Rather than our former ego, fear-based view of "me-against-the-world" experience, we feel somehow connected to everything and everyone we encounter.

Our lives come more and more into alignment with that perfect vision of Oneness. The more spiritually centered our lives become, the more they reflect joy, harmony and love. And where these are found, therein lies true freedom.

So, if you are weary of facing a world without meaning—of reacting, rather than proactively creating a life of peace and joy—may you experience the freedom of living in *Simply Spirit.*

17   Simply Love

*If love is in our heart, every
thought, word, and deed can bring
about a miracle.*

—Thich Nhat Hanh

"So, you're the 'happiness woman.' Does
that mean you're always happy?" the inter-
viewer asked, (referring to my first book,
Simply Happy), over a steamy cappuccino.
I just had to laugh out loud. I had recently
experienced a "hell day" and was eager to
answer this pointed question. I went on to
explain that perhaps 300 days the past
year I had lived in Heaven, i.e., living in
love, trusting that all things were working
through some divine plan toward the highest good. However, scattered randomly
throughout the year, the remaining 60-

some-odd days I had suffered through what I've come to call "hell days." Tormented by fear, judgment and depression I somehow lost touch with my child-like faith of the heavenly days.

After the interview I began wondering. What was the missing link? What was different about the times of torment? Then I remembered a night I had spent several years earlier that held the answer.

It was my third night camping alone in my new Rocky Mountain hideaway. The first two nights I was so overcome with awe and gratitude that the thought of fear never entered my mind. Both evenings, after a deliciously mindful meal, I had sat beside the rushing creek bundled up in warmth and wonder gently welcoming the night as the clear cerulean sky darkened to deep indigo. The stars had twinkled on one-by-one like tiny night-lights signaling that all was well.

The third evening I had become so involved in the menial task of cleaning up the gooey mess from a lotion spill in my duffel bag that I forgot about the approaching nightfall. After almost an hour of gingerly cleaning off bottles and such, I looked up suddenly. The darkness startled me. A shadow of fear moved over me. My heart-thump quickened in intensity. Soon the fear had overtaken me. I was in for a long night.

I was furious at myself for allowing something as useless as fear to steal my joy. I tried talking myself out of it. I knew that ultimately the choice for peace was up to me. Yet, coloring every thought with dark shadows, the fear seemed to be settling in for the night. Finally I remembered the angels. I had always loved the idea of these heavenly beings floating nearby in times of trouble, swooping down to save a stumbling soul.

Immediately and passionately I whispered, "God, send your holy angels to surround my tent tonight." The words ushered in a sweet peace. I gratefully prepared for

bed and went inside to tuck myself in. Smiling, I drifted off peacefully—knowing that
the celestial guards who hovered outside
my canvas cabin left me nothing to do but
safely slumber snuggled under flannel and
feathers on my Swedish cot. That was
around 10 o'clock.

Deep in the night, like the spontaneous
combustion of a balloon too close to heat, I
was thrown bolt-upright in bed. Horrified
by the sensation of being shaken awake by
someone inside my tent. Pulsating in sheer
terror, I cowered, paralyzed and dazed.
What was it? *Who* was it that woke me up?
Stunned by the explosion of palpable fear, I
grabbed the window flap to look out. Pure
panic gripped me as I witnessed the har-
rowing sight. Shimmering down the steep
hill behind my tent was a darting light,
dancing like a quivering flashlight of a
hunter hurrying toward the kill. What
kind of person would be up in the wilderness in the middle of the night unless they
were afraid of being seen in the light of

day? Yes, whoever this was had surely come to hurt me!

All of this terror transpired in a matter of seconds. "God, save me!" As the words burst desperately from my heart, I instantly remembered the angels. They were standing guard around my tent! I took a deep breath in an effort to calm myself. I spontaneously reached back to lift the veil away from the window and couldn't believe my eyes. I was looking up into the most incredible shimmering star-show I'd ever seen. I knew instantly it hadn't been a flashlight coming down the hill. The vibration of light I had glimpsed in fear was the pulsating energy of a universe full of only love for me.

I was so overcome by relief and awe that I walked fearlessly out into the brilliance. Like a trillion diamonds thrown across the black velvet sky, the wonder filled my heart with an inexpressible love. At that moment I was sure that the angels themselves had shaken me awake, making sure that I would not miss the unfolding miracle. The miracle was more than the incredible brilliance of the shimmering star-show. The real miracle was how at one moment I was consumed with fear and hopelessness and within a matter of moments I was filled to overflowing with a love that can only be described as radical.

I loved the starry sky, I loved the crashing creek waters, I loved my tent, the angels, my God, the entire universe and everyone, e-v-e-r-y-o-n-e in it. I knew that, at that moment, if someone walked up with a gun, rather than cringe in fear, I would surely say, "Welcome, stranger! What can I do for you?"

Radical, complete, *perfect love* filled me to overflowing. There was not enough room for even a trace of fear. I knew, for the first time in my life, what the scripture meant: *"Perfect love casteth out fear."* It was more than pretty words in an ancient book, but an undeniable truth that I had just come face to face with. All alone in the wilderness at ten thousand feet one extraordinary night I *experienced* the complete freedom of perfect love.

So, after such an awesome lesson, how is it that I still experience the occasional *hell day*? Because I forget about the angels. I forget about answered prayer. I forget that I cannot always see clearly. When I glare wildly into my dark night of the soul, consumed by fear, I can only see imagined demons hurrying down to harm me. If I would remember the angels, answered prayer, and the healing power of perfect love—then I would experience only heavenly days, no matter what chaotic circumstances I might find myself in.

I'm beginning to understand that the hell days are the days when I forget to love myself. Sometimes loving anything and anybody seems easier than loving ourselves. For whatever reasons, many of us arrive at adulthood with feelings of unworthiness and shame. Buying into the idea that we are somehow not worthy of perfect love, the seed of self-hatred and shame grows steadily into feelings of hopelessness, depression, worry, and guilt. Overcome with some or all of these devastating symptoms of self-loathing—sure that some dreadful vengeance is descending to destroy our very souls—we experience the damnation of fear.

Love, and only love, can save us from the hell days. Living in love causes us to miraculously shift to a deep trust that somehow things will work out regardless of how threatening life looks. Love leads us to the truth that we are perfectly safe and perfectly loved. The greatest freedom we can ever experience is to live in love. In love with ourselves, with God, with life and every soul—we are set free from the bondage of fear. The next time we feel ourselves descending into fear's fiery pit, let's remember instead to lift ourselves up, cry out for mercy and simply love.

I leave you with my wish for your freedom...

May you return to the child within who holds the dream of freedom in your heart...

To the knowledge that life is good and to be trusted. Return to the Spirit inside who knows that dreams are expressly for coming true.

May you dance and sing like nobody's listening, gleeful at the thought of the pure preciousness of each moment. Knowing that life is anything you believe it can be.

May you spread your wings and fly higher and higher in joy, peace and love. And know, dear child, that you never left the garden.

Suggested Reading

—*A Course in Miracles*, Glen Ellen. CA: Foundation for Inner Peace, Inc., 1975.

—*Conversations with God—Book I*, Neale Donald Walsch. G.P. Putman's Sons, 1995.

—*Creative Visualization*, Shakti Gawain. San Rafael, CA: New World Library, 1978.

—*God on a Harley*, Joan Brady. New York: Pocket Books, 1995.

—*Life's Companion*, Christina Baldwin. New York: Bantam Books, 1990.

—*Peace is Every Step*, Thich Nhat Hanh. New York: Bantam Books, 1991.

—*Revolution from Within*, Gloria Steinem. Boston: Little, Brown & Co., 1992.

—*Simple Abundance*, Sarah Ban Breathnach. New York: Warner Books, Inc., 1995.

—*Simply Happy*, Rebecca K. Merriman. Highland City, FL: Rainbow Books, Inc., 1996.

—*The Artist's Way,* Julia Cameron. New York: G.P. Putnam's Sons, 1992.

—*The Celestine Prophecy,* James Redfield. New York: Warner Books, Inc., 1993.

—*The Path of Transformation,* Shakti Gawain. Mill Valley, CA: Nataraj Publishing, 1993.

—*The Science of Mind,* Ernest Holmes. New York: G.P. Putnam's Sons, 1938.

—*The Seven Spiritual Laws of Success,* Deepak Chopra. San Rafael, CA: Amber-Allen Publishing, 1994.

—*Your Sacred Self,* Wayne W. Dyer. New York: HarperCollins Publishers, 1995.

About the Author

Rebecca K. Merriman, a former high school teacher, offers lively university courses and business seminars based on the ideas found in her books. She travels extensively as a popular motivational speaker.

Her *Simply Follow Your Bliss* retreats are held in exquisitely remote locales such as Yelapa, Mexico; Red Boiling Springs, TN; and Dzogchen, Ireland.

Ms. Merriman follows her bliss by spending her summers in the Colorado wilderness. The remainder of the year she lives simply in Tennessee in a cottage in the woods with her husband and three coddled cats.

For information on Rebecca's keynotes, seminars, retreats or cassette tapes, you may contact her at:

> Simply Happy Institute
> P.O. Box 10923
> Knoxville, TN 37939
> email: behappy@usit.net